THE
MINEOLA FAIR
THROUGH TIME

RICHARD PANCHYK

AMERICA
THROUGH TIME®
ADDING COLOR TO AMERICAN HISTORY

Acknowledgments

Thanks to Alan and Kena for their continued support and their dedication to my passion for local history. Thanks to Lizz and Matt for helping me explore the fair sites, past and present.

Image credits

Library of Congress: page 5, 13 (bottom), 19, 23 (bottom), 24, 25, 26, 27, 29, 30, 33, 38, 39 (bottom), 40, 41, 65 (top)
National Archives: page 42, 44,45, 46, 48, 50, 51
USGS: page 62, 63, 68 (bottom)
All other images courtesy of the author

America Through Time is an imprint of Fonthill Media LLC
www.through-time.com
office@through-time.com

Published by Arcadia Publishing by arrangement with Fonthill Media LLC
For all general information, please contact Arcadia Publishing:
Telephone: 843-853-2070
Fax: 843-853-0044
E-mail: sales@arcadiapublishing.com
For customer service and orders:
Toll-Free 1-888-313-2665

www.arcadiapublishing.com

First published 2022

Copyright © Richard Panchyk 2022

ISBN 978-1-63499-392-0

Typeset in Mrs Eaves XL Serif Narrow
Printed and bound in England

INTRODUCTION

Farming was a vital part of Long Island's history and many of its early settlers made their living off the land. From Queens (which once included what is today Nassau County) and Brooklyn all the way out through Suffolk, Long Island residents farmed—growing grains, fruit, and vegetables, and raising livestock. Despite the soil's sometimes rocky or sandy qualities, local production of agricultural products was critical especially in times when it was expensive and impractical to ship foodstuffs from elsewhere that might spoil anyway during transport. With so many people either involved in or dependent on one kind of farming or another, it made sense to hold some kind of event where farmers and citizens could come together to celebrate the bounty of the land, to exhibit and market their wares.

Agricultural fairs are an American tradition. Countless hundreds of villages, towns, counties, and states have held them over the years. These fairs began as a combination of business and pleasure, offering farmers and those in related industries (seed producers, wagon makers, farm equipment manufacturers, etc.) the chance to show off their wares as well as allowing the general public to enter competitions and enjoy exhibits, games, and races of all types. Over the years these fairs evolved as our country's (and in turn Long Island's) agricultural progress and predominance changed.

The history of fairs on Long Island goes back centuries. As early as 1693, there was an agricultural fair held in Jamaica, Queens. In the years that followed there were occasional fairs held in Jamaica and other locations (including Brooklyn), with prizes awarded for various outstanding produce and handcrafts. The fairs also introduced an element of circus or spectacle to draw spectators; during the 1728 fair at Jamaica, for example, a lion was on display.

In 1817, prominent citizens met at the old (since demolished) courthouse in Mineola at what is now Jericho Turnpike and Herricks Road, to discuss the idea of a permanent fair that would take place regularly rather than sporadically. In 1819, a fair was held at that site, and $200 was awarded in prizes for the various exhibits that ranged from potatoes to flannel. The fair was held again over the next three years but then the consistency faltered.

It was not until 1841 that a new attempt was made to implement a permanent, regular fair. A group of men met at William Niblo's Garden, a famous theater in Manhattan, and formed the Queens County Agricultural Society. Officers were elected and the society immediately set about arranging for its first fair, which was held on October 13, 1842, in the yard of a hotel in the village of Hempstead. The fair did well, with $250 being paid in prize money vs. $338 being taken in.

The fair led a nomadic existence during its first two decades, moving around between locations such as Flushing, Hempstead, and Jamaica. Horse racing was introduced at the 1851 fair in Jamaica and became a regular event. Plowing and spading competitions were another feature of early fairs. The 1859 fair took place in a field belonging to Richard Carman near the Hempstead Institute and brought in $18,000, up $7,000 over the previous year. The 1860 fair featured an address by Major M. R. Patrick, president of the New York State Agricultural College, of whom the Queens County Sentinel said: "He will deliver an address with which scholars and practical farmers will be equally satisfied."

The organizers of the fair desperately wanted it to have a permanent home. In 1865, there was much debate and discussion over the location of such a site. Ideally, it would be centrally located between Flushing, Jamaica, and Hempstead. The citizens of Hempstead pushed hard and got the town to donate land for the site in Mineola. So, when it came to a vote, the choice was between a 40-acre site that would be free or one that would cost $10,000 further west. Mineola won the vote and plans were soon made to build upon the site, located just south of Old Country Road and west of Washington Avenue.

The first fair at Mineola was held on September 27 and 28, 1866. The original fairgrounds included the exhibition hall that was said to have 1,000 windows (the hall cost $5,500), stables, business office, and pathways built at a total cost of $18,847.40, part of which was financed through donations. The exhibition hall had the equivalent of five rooms of 40 x 40 feet each, with 8,000 square feet of space altogether. According to Harper's Weekly of October 5, 1867: "The tables are so arranged that each department may be kept separate. In the centre is a tasty iron fountain, around which are tables for flowers. At one corner of the centre is the speaker's stand, from which position every person in the building can be seen; at another corner is the entrance to the ladies' saloon." The first permanent fair was a success. There were 170 horses on display and large crowds in attendance. The original grandstand could seat 1,000 people; it was replaced with a bigger one in 1894 to seat 2,000 people and was replaced again in 1910 after the previous one had burned down.

From the start, the Mineola fairgrounds were also used for other purposes; they were rented for a Republican Party rally and an army exercise later that same year. It must have been a welcome relief for exhibitors and fairgoers alike to know for certain that the next year's fair would definitely be in the same place. In 1867, there was also a one-day horticultural show in June that offered forty prizes, in addition to the regular and larger three-day autumn fair.

During the early days of the fair, each year seemed to bring new and exciting things. The highlight of the 1869 fair was a steam carriage invented by Richard Dudgeon, one he'd been working on for fourteen years. The first dog show of the fair was held in 1874, and baseball was introduced at the fair in 1875, while the last of the Shinnecock and Montauk Indians appeared at the fair in 1876. The first bicycle races at the fair were held in 1880.

Transportation to the fair was made easier by the existence of the railroad, but this mode of transportation was not without controversy. At first, the Long Island Rail Road did not charge for the shipment of animals to the fair, but in 1871 it was announced that a freight charge would apply. This did not go over well, and a competing railroad, the South Shore Railroad, offered to ship animals and exhibits free, so the LIRR ticket booth was kicked off the fairgrounds. The LIRR was back in the good graces of fair exhibitors by the end of the 1870s.

In the 1890s, the Mineola Fair took control of an additional 25 acres of land and developed a new landscaping plan and layout for the whole 65 acres they now controlled. The 1896 fair featured a great display of palm trees, some of which were twelve feet high, as well as pin cushions, pillows, paintings, needlework, scarves, quilts, and vases, among other things. There was also a dog show that occupied two large tents and featured a wide array of breeds on display. In addition, there was a collection of wagons and sleighs on display.

By the end of the nineteenth century, Queens County had become a part of New York City and Nassau County was born. Mineola became the county seat and construction of a grand county courthouse was begun just west of the fairgrounds. The Mineola Fair continued as it had, now located in a place of even greater importance.

At first, the fair organizers frowned upon the newfangled invention of the automobile. Until 1901, they were banned from the fairgrounds. In 1902, a special remote spot was begrudgingly set aside for their storage (parking). By 1905, though, cars were inevitable and popular, and the first automobile races were held at the Mineola Fair, followed by the first automobile show in 1908, and then the first airplane show in 1911, which was appropriate since famed aviator Glenn Curtiss had recently been using the field just across Washington Avenue from the fairgrounds.

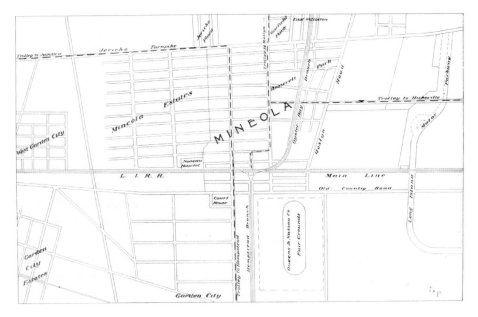

A 1908 map of the area around the fairgrounds in Mineola shows the undeveloped nature of the area; there were not even streets laid out in many spots at that time.

The fair's exhibitors in the early twentieth century were often a Who's Who of the rich and famous. According to the *Brooklyn Daily Eagle* of the 1912 Fair:

Samuel Willets of Roslyn has fine exhibits of wild fowl and Holstein cattle. Harry Payne Whitney wins the Charles H. Jones cup for the best bull at the fair. Robert Bacon of Westbury shows Guernseys. Clarence H. Mackay of Roslyn also has Guernseys. August Belmont gets first prize in Pearl Guinea hens. P. K. Hudson of East Norwich carries first prize for silver pheasants. In the horse show are represented such men as S. A. Warner of the Meadowbrook Hunt Club, Paul D. Cravath of Locust Valley, of the Piping Rock Club; David Dows of Jericho, Harold L. Goodwin of Roslyn, Thomas Hitchcock of Westbury, Harvey S. Ladew of Glen Cove, Thomas Le Boutillier of Westbury, Henry C. Phipps of Roslyn, and Howard Phipps and John S. Phipps of Westbury.

The fair was canceled in 1918 when the fairgrounds were utilized by the U.S. Army's nearby Camp Mills to serve as a base hospital, where thousands of sick soldiers were treated. Soon after, a base hospital complex was constructed just across Washington Avenue from the fairgrounds. The entire base hospital was empty of patients by early September 1919, however, and the 1919 fair could be held. In 1919, one fair highlight was an exhibit that was made by the Nassau County Mosquito Extermination Commission; 50,000 fairgoers "saw and heard some facts about mosquito extermination they never knew about" according to the *South Side Observer and Nassau Post* newspaper. Camp Mills was the "only camp in the United States where mosquito extermination was worked out so successfully, and the camp was free from the malaria germ."

In 1921, the display of automobiles at the fair was called "the best ever" using two big circus tents to display the latest and greatest in automotive technology. The headline in the *Daily Review* newspaper in advance of that year's fair proclaimed: "Better Racing, Bigger Purses, Faster Horses— Finer Horse Show—Greatest Exhibition of Blooded Cattle—Wonderful Displays of Handiwork—Snappiest Midway Ever Seen and Truly Delightful In Every Way."

The "Baby Show" became a very popular part of the Fair. A 1922 newspaper article in the *Daily Review* described that year's event:

The baby show will start on the second day of the fair, Sept. 27 and will continue on the 28th and 29th. Handsome prizes, 31 of them will be given in the different classes and they will range from a sewing machine for mother down to a string of beads for the little lassie who is winsome enough to carry off the prize. The classes for the baby contests and the prizes allotted are as follows: For the prettiest babies, five prizes, for the handsomest twin babies, five prizes; for the fattest babies, five prizes, for the smallest babies, five prizes; for doll babies, five prizes; and for the most strenuous babies, five prizes.

The 1929 Mineola Fair featured Fireman's Day, Farmers' Day, and Public Officials' Day. On Fireman's Day, there were various hose, hook and ladder, and pumping contests. On Farmers' Day there were speakers on seed sterilization, crop enemies, and fertilizer. On Public Officials' Day, politicians were on hand to meet and greet fairgoers. That year also saw a special "liberation of pigeons" where 1,000 pigeons were let go.

The 1933 fair netted $78,000 during its five days and saw 15,000 visitors on a single day. One of its highlights was the so-called World's Worst Automobile Race, the Ash Can Derby, featuring automotive relics. On Wednesday of the fair that year, Nassau County schools were closed so children could attend the fair. Daredevils staged head-on crashes at 40 mph for a shocked audience. The 1934 Mineola Fair again featured automobile daredevils, as well as a Nassau police parade and drill, a circus and rodeo, and a nightly stage show.

Meanwhile, by early 1935 there were calls for a new courthouse to replace the old one that was near the fairgrounds. In the fall of 1937, Hempstead township citizens voted to give 40 acres of the Mineola Fair site to Nassau County upon which to build a new courthouse. An additional 22 acres were purchased from the Queens-Nassau Agricultural society and a final eight acres were purchased from the Garden City company to complete county ownership of all land bounded by Old Country Road, Washington Avenue, Eleventh Street, and the Mineola-Garden City railroad spur. When the original deal was announced in 1937, it was thought that the fair had seen its last days in Mineola. But soon after, an agreement was reached to allow the fair to continue on the rest of the property not used by county administrative buildings, until 1948.

The Mineola Fair went on through the 1940s. During wartime, things took on a serious air, notably with a 1942 speech by Queens borough president James Burke, who spoke before a grandstand crowd of 2,500 people and warned that Long Island could be the focal point for an enemy attack and urged citizens to form a civilian defense organization for the protection of Long Island residents.

Through the years and changing times, everyone always seemed glad for the fair's continued existence. A 1948 editorial in the *Hempstead Sentinel* explained: "Instead of dwindling on the vine, the Fair has become more robust with the passage of time. Now many industrial and commercial firms have joined the ranks of farmers and animal breeders as exhibitors, making the Fair larger in scope and more representative of the changing nature of Nassau County."

Ultimately the Mineola Fair lasted in Mineola until 1952, when the winds of change could no longer be held off. The fair went out in Mineola with a bang. A newspaper headline after day 1 of the fair that September read: "45,000 Jam Mineola Fair For Best Opener in Years." Some of the highlights that year were the "Three-Legged Chicken" a lady sword swallower, a sheep-headed man (?!) and the "fat girl and the thin man."

With the fair forced to leave, the organizers wanted to find a new home quickly so that they did not miss a year. Two possibilities for its relocation were the former Salisbury Golf Club, which had become Salisbury Park (currently known as Eisenhower Park) in East Meadow or the 275-acre Roosevelt Raceway property in Westbury. The latter was chosen as the new site of the Mineola Fair, which was combined with the Nassau Industrial Exhibition to become the Mineola Fair and Industrial Exposition. The new location had one big advantage over the Mineola site—it had ample parking (for 10,000 cars!), where in Mineola parking was always an issue. The 1953 fair included an exhibition by local aircraft manufacturers of their latest weaponry, while IBM showed a "mechanical brain" for the first time on Long Island. The 1953 fair spanned over nine days and was the first time in the fair's history that it was on two Sundays.

The 1954 Mineola Fair featured something called Anniversary Day as its opener on September 8, with descendants present of some of the well-known Long Island families who started the first of the fairs that would become the Mineola Fair. Sunday was Family Day, with musical star and Long Island resident Guy Lombardo. Its closing day the following Sunday was Citizenship Day, where 1,000 new American citizens took their oath of allegiance in front of Nassau County judges.

The Mineola Fair was canceled in 1955 due to the construction of the New York State Thruway in Yonkers near the Yonkers Raceway; the Yonkers Raceway had an agreement with Roosevelt Raceway that each would serve as the other's emergency racetrack location, and with the uncertainty of nearby construction the Westbury site had to be kept available for potential use. As it turned out the Yonkers Raceway decided it would be able to hold its regular track season, but by then it was too late to pull together a fair on short notice.

The fairs held at Roosevelt Raceway took full advantage of the racetrack there. In 1958, for example, there was a sports car race for teams made entirely of employees of industrial firms on Long Island, including Sperry Rand, Grumman Aircraft, Republic Aircraft, and Long Island Lighting, among others. There was also a Roman Chariot Race. According to a newspaper article in the *Northport Observer*: "Authentic ancient war chariots and fiery steeds will be the racing equipment for the daredevils who will contest in this oldest of horse races." A total of $15,000 in cash prizes were offered for the various contests that year.

The 1960 fair had themes such as American heritage, transportation, education in the space age, security and world peace, and government, and drew a total of 200,000 visitors and had 300 exhibits. In 1962 the name was changed to the Long Island Fair, and the fair that year featured sky divers from the U.S. Army Parachute Team, who made jumps from altitudes ranging from 3,000 feet to as high as 20,000 feet, free falling for a while before opening their black and gold parachutes, for a landing on a target circle on the racetrack.

In 1963, the fair was held from August 24 to September 2, the first time in many years the entirety of the fair did not occur during the months of September and October. About 130,000 people attended the fair that year. In 1964, the Fair was skipped on account of and in deference to the World's Fair in Flushing, Queens.

A highlight of the 1966 fair's ten-day run was a parade and a chorus of thousands of Girl Scouts singing on International Girl Scout Day. That year also featured country square dancing and Hawaiian flame and knife dancing.

An opportunity for relocation and second rebirth of the fair was born with Nassau County's acquisition of a 165-acre farm property on the Nassau-Suffolk County border in 1963, which was to be used to create a living history farm village featuring old buildings transported there from around Long Island. The fair moved to the Old Bethpage site in 1970. In moving to Old Bethpage, the fair returned to a more bucolic atmosphere that had been lacking since about the third or fourth decade of the twentieth century, when development began to encroach on the Mineola site. One thing the Old Bethpage site had in common with its previous location in Westbury was that it was a shared site not strictly dedicated to the fair, and the site was open year-round by its host. The 209-acre Old Bethpage Village Restoration is an all-seasons celebration of the life in the nineteenth-century days when agriculture was more prevalent in the western half of Long Island. Since the Village has a working farm, it seems even more appropriate that the Long Island Fair is located there.

The first Old Bethpage fair in 1970 did not have any animal exhibits, but it included plowing, spading, fiddling, and kite-flying contests, an old-time fashion show, folk singing, and the usual exhibition of prize-winning vegetables, handcrafts, and flowers. The 1971 fair had an interesting attraction: a balloon daredevil named Professor Waligunda who rose over the fairgrounds in his red, white, and blue balloon before a thrilled crowd.

The 1975 Long Island Fair's special attraction was "Viktor," a 350-pound "ferocious wrestling bear, direct from the northlands and set to provide a unique animal act typical of special attractions in rural towns during the early 1880s." There were also recreations of the nineteenth-century presidential political campaigns of William Henry Harrison and Martin Van Buren. The price of admission that year was $2.25 for adults and $1.50 for children.

In 1983, the Nassau County Department of Parks and Recreation's Museum Division put out a call for old photographs of the original long-since demolished exhibition hall at the Mineola site of the fair to help them build a reconstruction of the historic building at the Old Bethpage site. The replica that stands on the fairgrounds today is definitely a living homage to the early days of the fair.

The year 2020 was a wash with the Covid pandemic canceling the Long Island Fair, but it was back in 2021. In 2020, the Nassau County Legislature authorized the Agricultural Society to use the Old Bethpage site for the next ten years, assuring the continuance of a long and storied tradition. The legislature also authorized grants to fund $364,000 worth of improvements and repairs to the exhibit hall and other structures. The modern Long Island Fair is still very popular, bringing visitors from far and wide to enjoy the two-day festivities.

Meanwhile, Queens County has also been holding its own fair for several decades, at the Queens County Farm Museum in Glen Oaks (a working farm and historical site near the Nassau County border), offering similar activities and exhibits as the Long Island Fair. Both fairs are proof that there is still great interest in celebrating and preserving the farming heritage and old-time fun spirit of the original nineteenth-century fairs.

The very first Queens County Agricultural Fair took place on October 13, 1842, in Hempstead Village. It was held in the yard of R. G. Anderson's Hotel. There was a parade to the Methodist Church, seen here in an early *c.* 1960s photograph (and still standing today), where a speech was made by William T. McConn, the vice chancellor of New York State. The receipts at the fair amounted to $338, while the payout in premiums was $250; the fair was profitable.

ODE FOR AN AGRICULTURAL CELEBRATION.

Far back in the ages,
   The plough with wreaths was crowned;
The hands of kings and sages
   Entwined the chaplet round;
Till men of spoil disdained the toil
   By which the world was nourished,
And dews of blood enriched the soil
   Where green their laurels flourished:
—Now the world her fault repairs—
   The guilt that stains her story;
And weeps her crimes amid the cares
   That formed her earliest glory.

The proud throne shall crumble,
   The diadem shall wane,
The tribes of earth shall humble
   The pride of those who reign;
And War shall lay his pomp away;—
   The fame that heroes cherish,
The glory earned in deadly fray
   Shall fade, decay, and perish.
Honour waits, o'er all the Earth,
   Through endless generations,
The art that calls her harvests forth,
   And feeds the expectant nations.

At the Methodist Church, an agricultural ode specially composed for the occasion by the famous New York writer and newspaper editor William Cullen Bryant (1794-1878) was sung.

The fair was held at the same location in Hempstead in 1843, and then in 1844 it moved to Jamaica, where part of the festivities were held in the Presbyterian Church there, built in 1813 and seen here *c.* 1905. The church still stands today; in 1920 it was moved from its original location at 163rd Street to 164th Street. The church was organized in 1662.

How happy is the husbandman!

More happy than a king!
For, after all, a diadem

Is an uneasy thing;
And the hero with his laurels

All fresh upon his brow,
Is not so light of heart as he

Who whistles at the plough.

Then God be with our pleasant land,

And give us men of worth,
To cultivate and understand

The treasures of the earth:
And blessings on our native soil;

Forever may it be
The heritage of plenteousness,

For hands unstained and free.

In 1843, another agricultural ode by William Cullen Bryant (seen here in a daguerreotype from the 1850s) was sung at the fair, this time in a tent at the fairgrounds in Hempstead.

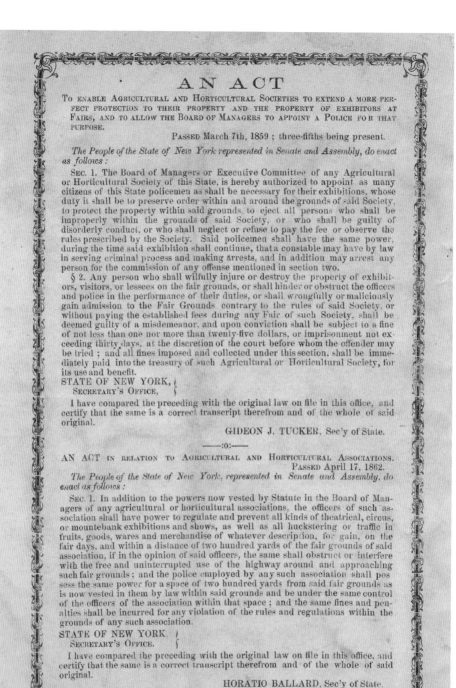

AN ACT

To ENABLE AGRICULTURAL AND HORTICULTURAL SOCIETIES TO EXTEND A MORE PER-
FECT PROTECTION TO THEIR PROPERTY AND THE PROPERTY OF EXHIBITORS AT
FAIRS, AND TO ALLOW THE BOARD OF MANAGERS TO APPOINT A POLICE FOR THAT
PURPOSE.

PASSED March 7th, 1859 ; three-fifths being present.

The People of the State of New York represented in Senate and Assembly, do enact as follows :

SEC. 1. The Board of Managers or Executive Committee of any Agricultural or Horticultural Society of this State, is hereby authorized to appoint as many citizens of this State policemen as shall be necessary for their exhibitions, whose duty it shall be to preserve order within and around the grounds of said Society, to protect the property within said grounds, to eject all persons who shall be improperly within the grounds of said Society, or who shall be guilty of disorderly conduct, or who shall neglect or refuse to pay the fee or observe the rules prescribed by the Society. Said policemen shall have the same power, during the time said exhibition shall continue, that a constable may have by law in serving criminal process and making arrests, and in addition may arrest any person for the commission of any offense mentioned in section two.

§ 2. Any person who shall wilfully injure or destroy the property of exhibitors, visitors, or lessees on the fair grounds, or shall hinder or obstruct the officers and police in the performance of their duties, or shall wrongfully or maliciously gain admission to the Fair Grounds contrary to the rules of said Society, or without paying the established fees during any Fair of such Society, shall be deemed guilty of a misdemeanor, and upon conviction shall be subject to a fine of not less than one nor more than twenty-five dollars, or imprisonment not exceeding thirty days, at the discretion of the court before whom the offender may be tried ; and all fines imposed and collected under this section, shall be immediately paid into the treasury of such Agricultural or Horticultural Society, for its use and benefit.

STATE OF NEW YORK, {
SECRETARY'S OFFICE, }

I have compared the preceding with the original law on file in this office, and certify that the same is a correct transcript therefrom and of the whole of said original.

GIDEON J. TUCKER, Sec'y of State.

——:o:——

AN ACT IN RELATION TO AGRICULTURAL AND HORTICULTURAL ASSOCIATIONS.
PASSED April 17, 1862.

The People of the State of New York, represented in Senate and Assembly, do enact as follows :

SEC. 1. In addition to the powers now vested by Statute in the Board of Managers of any agricultural or horticultural associations, the officers of such association shall have power to regulate and prevent all kinds of theatrical, circus, or mountebank exhibitions and shows, as well as all huckstering or traffic in fruits, goods, wares and merchandise of whatever description, for gain, on the fair days, and within a distance of two hundred yards of the fair grounds of said association, if in the opinion of said officers, the same shall obstruct or interfere with the free and uninterrupted use of the highway around and approaching such fair grounds ; and the police employed by any such association shall possess the same power for a space of two hundred yards from said fair grounds as is now vested in them by law within said grounds and be under the same control of the officers of the association within that space ; and the same fines and penalties shall be incurred for any violation of the rules and regulations within the grounds of any such association.

STATE OF NEW YORK, {
SECRETARY'S OFFICE. }

I have compared the preceding with the original law on file in this office, and certify that the same is a correct transcript therefrom and of the whole of said original.

HORATIO BALLARD, Sec'y of State.

Two New York State laws, passed in 1859 and 1862, protecting agricultural societies and fairs, authorized the punishment of anyone who would "injure or destroy the property of exhibitors, visitors, or lessees on the fair grounds." This apparently must have been an issue, or such laws would not have been necessary.

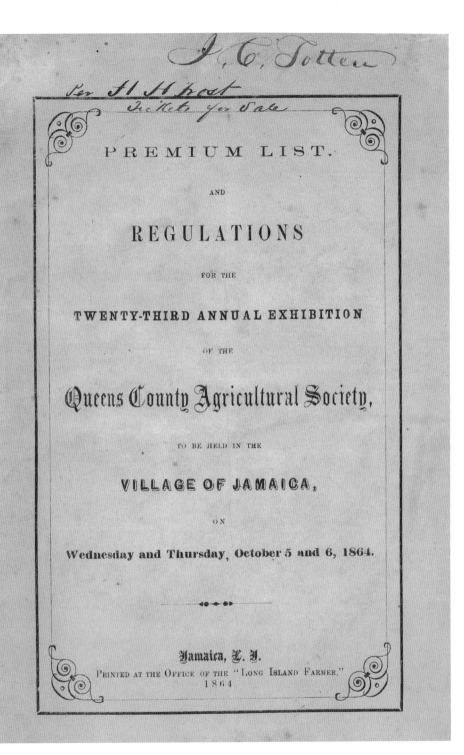

PREMIUM LIST.

AND

REGULATIONS

FOR THE

TWENTY-THIRD ANNUAL EXHIBITION

OF THE

Queens County Agricultural Society,

TO BE HELD IN THE

VILLAGE OF JAMAICA,

ON

Wednesday and Thursday, October 5 and 6, 1864.

Jamaica, L. I.

PRINTED AT THE OFFICE OF THE "LONG ISLAND FARMER,"
1864

Cover of the "Premium List and Regulations for the Twenty-Third Annual Exhibition of the Queens County Agricultural Society, to be Held in the Village of Jamaica on Wednesday and Thursday, October 5 and 6, 1864." Just two years later, the fair would find a permanent home in Mineola after a nomadic existence for its first twenty-five years.

Terms of Admission to Grounds.

--:--o--:--

All Life and Annual Members with their families under twenty-one years of age will be admitted on presenting their tickets at the entrance.

Life Member's Tickets, - - - - - - - - - - - $10 *each.*
Exhibitors and Annual Members, - - - - - - - - 1 *each.*

Their tickets will enable the owner to pass in and out at the proper gate (by showing the ticket,) during the exhibition, and to enter any number of articles for exhibition.

Single Tickets of Admission, - - - - - - - - 25 *cents.*
Children under 12 years of age, - - - - - - 10 *cents.*
Carriage in charge of a driver each time of entry, - - 2 *dollars.*
Each person in Carriage, (except members,) - - - 25 *cents.*

No Return Checks will be Given.

No horses shall be allowed to be hitched or tied upon the grounds, and shall remain in charge of the driver, in the place designated by the Superintendent, and no riding or driving will be allowed on the track.

Terms of admission to the fairgrounds and instructions to judges, from the 1864 Premium List and Regulations for the fair in Jamaica, Queens. An admission ticket to the 1864 fair was twenty-five cents; ten cents for children twelve and under. The admission price for adults to the 2021 Long Island Fair was $20.

General Instructions to Judges.

--:--o--:--

The Judges on the various articles will meet at 10 o'clock, A. M., on Wednesday, October, 5th, and proceed immediately to the discharge of their duties.

Persons who are named as Judges to award premiums, and who do not intend to serve as such, will please inform the Secretary, that the Committee may be kept full.

The Committee of Judges will please report any article of merit to which they shall not have awarded a premium, but which they may regard as worthy of notice ; and they are desired also to withhold premiums from any article of inferior merit, though there be no competition.

The Judges are desired to pay particular attention to the regulations and requirements in the premium list, and upon the Judges' Books.

The Judges are requested to return the books containing their award, to the Secretary's office as early as possible.

No person will be allowed to interfere with the Judges while in the discharge of their duties ; and any person interfering by letter or otherwise, will be excluded from competition.

The Judges are expressly instructed to exclude *overfed fat animals*, as the object of the Society is to have superior animals. suited for breeding purposes.

All fruits, flowers, plants, and vegetables, offered for competition for premiums, must be grown by the competitor.

Should any individual enter an animal or article in another name than that of the *bona fide owner*, the person making such entry shall not be allowed a premium should one be reported by the Judges, and shall be precluded from competing at any other Exhibition of the Society

------- :--o--: -------

PREMIUMS FOR 1864.

—:-o-:—

The Premiums will be delivered according to the printed list, unless notice is given to the Treasurer of a desired change in money or books as awarded, within ten days after the Exhibition.

CLASS I.

Cattle—Short Horns.

BULLS.

Best bull, over 3 years old, $10
2d do................5
3d do................2
Best bull, 2 years old,.......10
2d do................5
3d do................2
Best bull, 1 year old........10
2d do................5
3d do................2
Best cow, over 5 years old,..10
2d do................5
3d do................2
Best heifer, 2 years old.....10
2d do................5
3d do................2
Best heifer, 1 year old......10
2d do................5
3d do................2

Devons.

Best bull, over 3 years old,..10
2d do................5
3d do................2
Best bull, 2 years old....10
2d do................5
3d do................2
Best bull, 1 year old........10
2d do................5
3d do................2
Best cow, over 3 years old...10
2d do................5
3d do................2
Best heifer, 2 years old......10
2d do................5
3d do................2
Best heifer, 1 year old......10
2d do................5
3d do................2

Ayrshires.

Best bull, over 3 years old..10
2d do................5
3d do................2
Best bull, 2 years old.......10
2d do................5
3d do................2
Best bull, 1 year old........10
2d do................5
3d do................2
Best cow, over 3 years old,..10
2d do................5
3d do................2
Best heifer, 2 years old......10
2d do................5
3d do................2
Best heifer, 1 year old......10
2d do................5
3d do................2

Alderneys.

Best bull, over 3 years old,..10
2d do................5
3d do................2
Best bull, 2 years old.......10
2d do................5
3d do................2
Best bull, 1 year old........10
2d do................5
3d do................2
Best cow, over 3 years old...10
2d do................5
3d do................2
Best heifer, 2 years old......10
2d do................5
3d do................2
Best heifer, 1 year old,......10
2d do................5
3d do................2

JUDGES—Wm. Floyd Jones, Benj. L. Swan, Jr., Valentine Hallock, Robert Morrell, Sylvanus S. Riker.

A list of some of the premiums offered for bulls in the 1864 Queens County Agricultural Society Fair. The fair was heavy on animals, with this particular one offering prizes for bulls, cows, horses, mules, ponies, sheep, pigs, pheasants, ducks, turkeys, and pigeons.

CLASS 13.

Flowers.

Best floral design or orna-
ment,.................$10
2d do......................5
3d do......................3
Best collection of house plants
in pots, not less than 10
different specimens,.....5
2d do......................3
Best variety cut flowers,....5
2d do......................3
Best collection of asters,....5
2d do......................3
Best show of phloxes,.......5
2d do......................3
Best collection of monthly car-
nations,................5
2d do......................3
Best show of verbenas,......5
2d do......................3
Best show of roses,.........5
2d do......................3
Best assortment of newest variety of dahlias, not less
than 12 dissimilar blooms,
with names,...........5
2d do......................3
Best pair parlor boquets.....5
Best pair hand boquets.....5
2d do......................3
Best display of newly introduced flowers,..........5
2d do......................3

All articles (except cut flowers,)
should be arranged on the tables on
Tuesday, the 4th of October, cut
flowers and boquets before 9 o'clock
on the morning of October 5th.

JUDGES.—John A. King, Jr., Charles
H. Rogers, Wm. D. F. Manice, John
W. Degrauw, Charles N. Doane.

CLASS 14.

Domestic Manufac-
tures.

Best and greatest variety of
Domestic Manufactures,
the work of the exhibi-
tor, made in the county,
....pair silver butter knives
and dip.

Best variety of work by a girl
under 21 years of age,
....pair silver butter knives
Best patchwork quilts by girls
under 12 years of age,..
.......silver butter knife.
Best pair of woollen socks for
gentlemen, by girls un-
der 12 years of age,....
.......silver butter knife.
Best quilted bed spread, ...2
Best knit bed spread,.......2
Best hearth rug,........ ...1
Best pair woolen blankets,..1
Best pair woolen stockings,.1
Best pair cotton stockings,..1
Best pair linen stockings,...1
Best pair silk stockings,....1
Best sample of woolen cloth,.1
Best   "   woolen carpet 1
Best   "   rag carpet,..1
Best   "   flannel, ...1
Best   "   linen cloth,..1
Best   "   linen thread,.1
Best   "   woolen thread 1
Best   "   linen diaper,.1

Articles of domestic manufacture to
be made in the family within the year.

JUDGES.—Mrs. Job Jackson, Mrs. A.
A. Degrauw, Mrs. M. R. Striker, Mrs.
S. L. Spader, Mrs. Mary Story.

CLASS 15.

Needle Work

Best plain shirt, without em-
broidering, made by a la-
dy over 21 years of age,
..pair silver butter knives.
2d do.......silver butter knife.

Best plain shirt, without em-
broidering, made by a
girl under 21 years, of age
..pair silver butter knives
and dip.
2d do.......silver butter knife,

Best evidence of taste and skill
in any kind of needle
work or embroidery, by
any girl under 14 years
of age,...pair silver knives
and dip.

This page from the 1864 premium list shows some of the other categories of entries which were available.
Note the prizes for some are silver butter knives, instead of money.

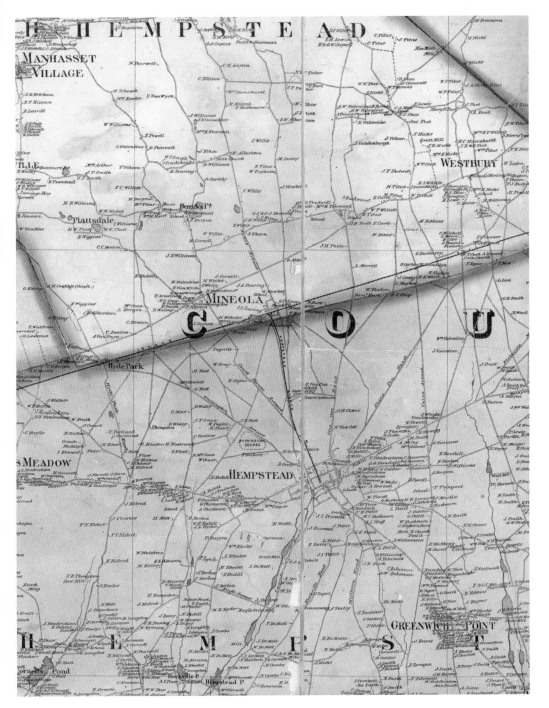

A map of Long Island in 1859, just before the fair moved to its new permanent home, shows a sparsely populated Mineola and surrounding areas.

The exhibit hall building is the highlight in this 1867 drawing of the recently completed fairgrounds at Mineola. The image seems to show organized chaos in the approach to the grounds. The accompanying story

in *Harper's Weekly* says that year's fair was "a fair illustration of what educated farmers, modern machines, and improved tillage can accomplish" even in "beds of coarse sand and gravel" like the Hempstead Plains.

Some winners at the Mineola Fair took their entries on to the New York State Fair. Seen here, cattle judging at the State Fair in Syracuse *circa* 1905.

Mineola was a country village when the Queens County Agricultural Society decided to give its annual fair a permanent home there. This view looks east from a windmill on Searing Avenue.

Despite its quiet semi-rural existence, Mineola was soon to become a hopping place. William K. Vanderbilt, Jr.'s Vanderbilt Cup Automobile Races were a huge draw to Mineola in the early twentieth century. Vanderbilt was an early automobile enthusiast who used local roads as the course for his races. This image shows a view of Krug's Hotel in downtown Mineola during the Vanderbilt Cup Race in 1906. The hotel was on the race course in the 1904, 1905, and 1906 races.

The Ladies' Kennel Association of America held their Sixth Annual Summer Dog Show at the Mineola Fairgrounds June 4 and 5, 1908. In this photograph, Marion C. Bourne stands with "Michael Strogoff" voted the best American-bred Russian Wolf Hound at the dog show.

Big society names were present at the annual dog show. In this image from 1908, Mrs. Morris Mandy holds Mrs. J. P. Morgan's Pekinese "Pou-sa."

OPPOSITE PAGE:

Above: Mr. & Mrs. Tyler Morse with their Old English sheep dogs, "Dame Dorris" and "Endcliffe Majestic," at the dog show in Mineola on June 5, 1908. The dog show was a popular event at the fairgrounds; in 1909 there were 600 entrants and in 1910 there were 860 entrants. A fairgrounds building is visible in the background.

Below: M. R. Guggenheim and his "Eskimo dogs," aka huskies, at the 1908 Mineola Dog Show.

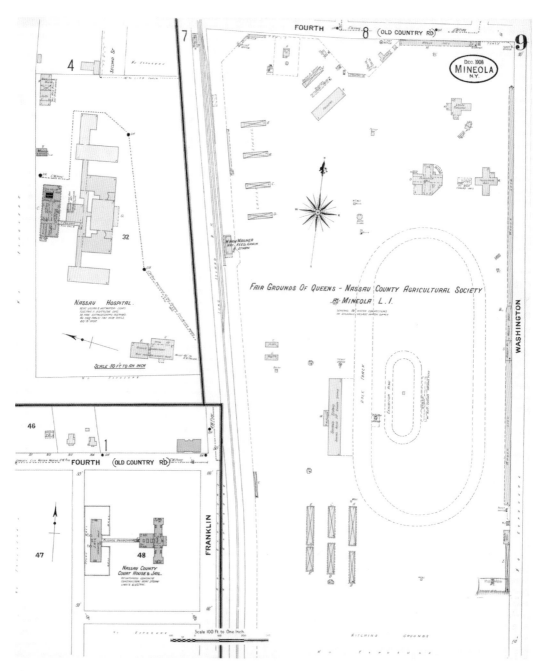

The 1908 Sanborn Fire Insurance Map of the fairgrounds gives an accurate view of the buildings on the property. Fire insurance maps were especially important in the days when most buildings were wood frame and heat was generated by burning wood or coal.

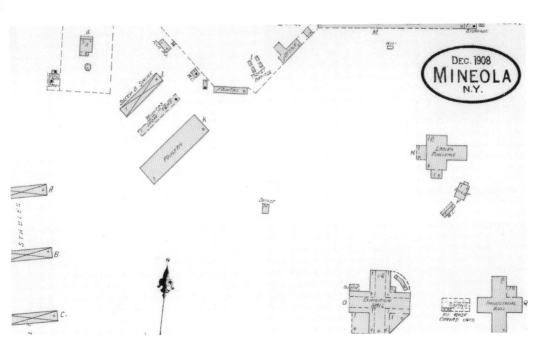

Close-ups of the 1908 Sanborn map reveal details of the fairground buildings at that time.

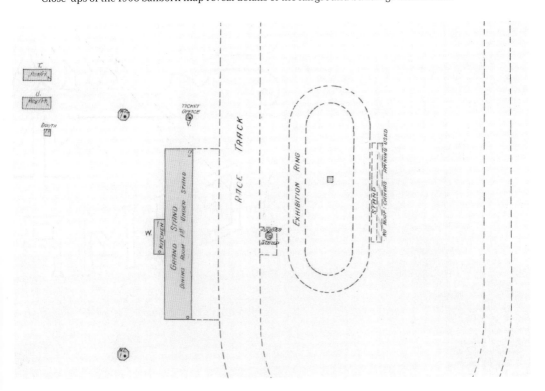

6037   THE DENTON BUILDING MINEOLA, L. I.

The Denton Building, an office building on Old Country Road just west of the Mineola fairgrounds, was at the time of this image (1908) the headquarters for the Vanderbilt Cup Races, the course for which varied from year to year but in 1906 ran through Mineola along Jericho Turnpike.

Advertisements for four Mineola hotels in 1908. As the county seat and the site of the Mineola Fair, and also on or near the Vanderbilt Cup Race track, people had reason to stay overnight. Once aviation came to Mineola the following year, visitors had yet another reason to find accommodations.

The arrival to Mineola of the noted aviator pioneer Glenn Curtiss in 1909 was a big deal. Curtiss was seeking a good location to fly in the New York City area and settled on the Hempstead Plains as the ideal spot. His first airfield was located directly across the street from the Mineola fairgrounds.

When Glenn Curtiss came to Long Island in 1909, he set up a flying field across Washington Avenue from the Mineola Fairgrounds, just east of it. It was from this field that he set a new flight record and won the Scientific American Trophy for the longest airplane flight. On July 13, 1909, he flew his plane for 2 miles. The next day he flew it 5 miles, on the 15th for 6 miles, on the 16th for 15 miles, and a day later he flew a total distance of 29 miles, including 15 miles at one time. He won a $10,000 prize for his efforts. At top is Curtiss' plane in Mineola, and at bottom a crowd of people gathers around his plane in at the flying field in Mineola.

With the advent of aviation in the area, Peter McLaughlin's Gold Bug Hotel in downtown Mineola quickly became known (thanks to his quick marketing efforts) as an "aviation hotel," the home for pioneer flyers.

One of the trolleys that used to crisscross the streets of a thriving town of Mineola in the early twentieth century, seen here on Main Street.

THE PHONOGRAPH.

TRYING HIS LUNGS.

WHEELMAN'S PARADISE.

THE 2:40 CLASS.

A LITTLE BIT IN COLOR.

SEEING THE ELEPHANT.

THE FLOWER SHOW.

ON THE MIDWAY.

SCENES AT A COUNTRY FAIR.

MINEOLA, LONG ISLAND.

Various scenes from the Mineola Fair during the early twentieth century.

The race track and grandstand of the Mineola Fair as seen *c.* 1910. A poem about the fair appeared in a 1912 edition of the *Brooklyn Daily Eagle*: "Cutie," the cop/Gives his arms a flop/And the wheels begin to spin/And the horses gay/In fine array/Come dancing, prancing in/The sun comes out/And you hear 'em shout/While the prize bulls rip and tear/And the pop-eyed goose/And the crowds cut loose/At the Mineola Fair."

Circa 1910, a racing ostrich at the Mineola fairgrounds. The fair usually had some oddball event or another designed to attract spectators.

A view of the fairgrounds *c.* 1910 shows various tents set up for exhibits.

A *c.* 1910 view of the cruciform-shaped exhibition building at the Mineola Fair. It was demolished by the mid-twentieth century, before the fair left Mineola. A reconstruction of this building was erected at the fair's current site in Old Bethpage (it was completed in 1995).

A "Fakir's Row" at the Mineola Fair *c.* 1910s. Fakirs were supposed holy men with special powers but were more likely just con men selling ordinary wares to fairgoers. Note this postcard refers to it as the Nassau County Fair.

A women's suffrage march passes through downtown Mineola on May 25, 1913.

Nassau Hospital, Mineola, L I.

Unlike many of its neighboring towns, the Mineola of old had a hospital. Nassau Hospital was founded in 1896 and was one of Long Island's earliest modern hospitals. Now known as NYU Winthrop Hospital (it became affiliated with NYU Langone Medical Center in 2017), it has 591 beds and has grown far beyond its humble beginnings. While the present-day hospital looks nothing like its predecessor, the history is proudly displayed— there is a large, vintage marble plaque listing the original donors mounted on the wall inside the main building.

An embossed rose postcard addressed to Bessie from the Mineola Fair. The fair was widely known and a destination worthy of sending one's greetings from.

Theodore Roosevelt leaving the old courthouse near the fairgrounds in an undated photo. Roosevelt was present in 1900 as governor of New York, to lay the cornerstone for the courthouse. Roosevelt visited the fair in 1899 but reports said he was not that impressed.

An early twentieth-century photograph of Shaw & Son Practical Horse Shoers, which would likely have seen a good amount of business from the Mineola Fair given the number of horses on display and in races there.

When Nassau County was created in 1899, Mineola became the county seat, and the quiet town was assured of a certain degree of importance and activity. Media attention was drawn to Mineola during notable trials such as the 1914 trial of Mrs. Florence Conklin Carman for the murder of Lulu Bailey. At top is Mrs. Carman's maid, Celia Coleman, who testified that she heard her employer confess to the murder. At bottom on the courthouse steps is the jury: the foreman, Robert F. Ludlam, standing on the left, and Alois Angler, Frank Mount, William Hovey, March Gottsch, Alvin Smith, James Giraud, Jacob Anton, John Molyneaux, Joseph Ashton, Eugene Carpenter, and Charles Stryker.

After a day at the fair, visitors could spend some time in downtown Mineola, and perhaps stop at Ehrichs General Store, where they could find everything from charcoal to carriages.

The Nassau County Courthouse as it appeared in 1917. The fairgrounds were to the right of this image.

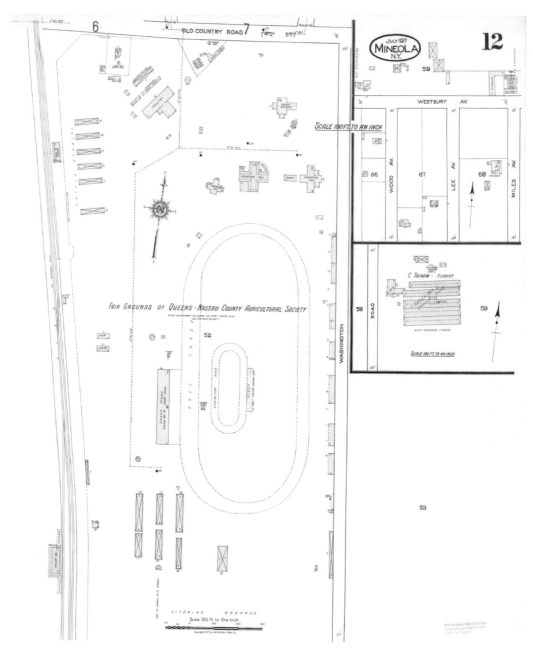

The 1917 Sanborn Fire Insurance Map of the fairgrounds shows a marked difference from the 1908 map. Many more buildings have since been added and the land across Washington Avenue has been partly developed.

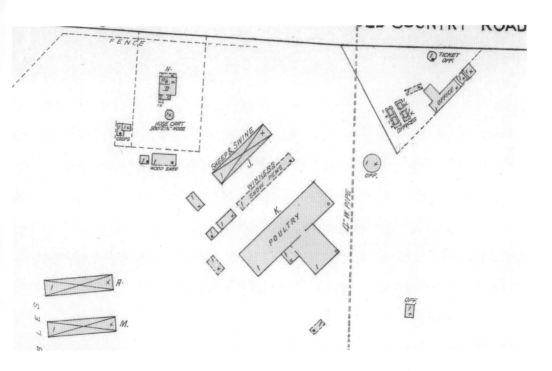

Details from the 1917 Sanborn map show the various buildings on the fairground's property.

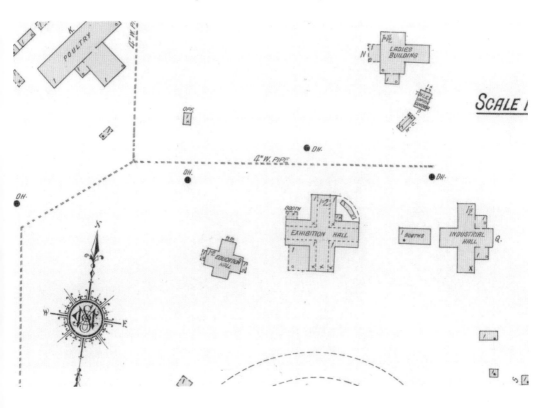

An undated early twentieth-century image showing some officials gathered near the grandstand at the fair.

OPPOSITE PAGE:

Airplanes in the sky were a common sight over Mineola, especially during 1917 and 1918, when Hazelhurst Field (what was to become Roosevelt Field) was used by the Army to train pilots for the war. Seen here are planes in battle formation.

A regiment of the 42nd (Rainbow) Division at the Mineola Fair in 1917. According to military publicity, "the best feature at Nassau County Fair, Mineola, Long Island, was the drill put on by the 165th Infantry, formerly the old 69th New York National Guard, now training for service at Camp Mills, near Mineola."

For a brief time in 1918, some of the fairground's buildings were occupied by the U.S. Army and used for the Camp Mills Evacuation Hospital. Camp Mills itself was to the southeast. In May 1918, an Evacuation Hospital complex was constructed across Washington Avenue from the southern end of the fairgrounds. These photographs were taken on July 21, 1919.

More than a dozen hospital buildings, connected by walkways, were located adjacent to the Mineola Fairgrounds, in what is now considered Garden City. Though construction was only completed in February 1919, the hospital was abandoned by the end of 1919. At top is the bacteriological laboratory, and at bottom is a 100-bed general ward.

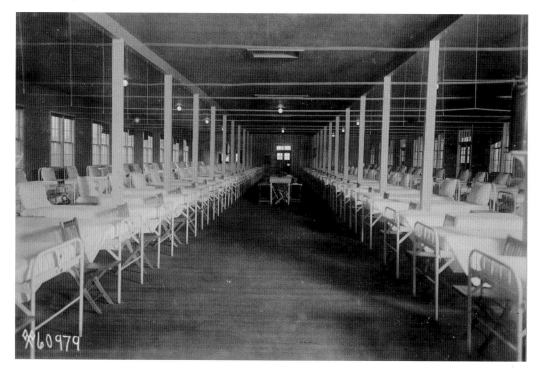

Prize ribbons for first and second place pigeons at the 1930 Mineola Fair. Red and blue ribbons are used at the fair to this day to denote winning exhibits.

A 1931 aerial view of Mineola taken from 5,000 feet shows a detailed view of the Mineola Fairgrounds. The old Nassau County Courthouse is just left of the fairgrounds. Numerous buildings can be seen on the northern end of the property while the southern half is largely taken up by the racetrack.

Then Governor Franklin D. Roosevelt addresses a gathered crowd while campaigning at the Mineola Fairgrounds on November 5, 1932, just before Election Day when he would be elected the next president of the United States.

The Roosevelt Raceway in its earliest incarnation, as a home to the 1936 George Vanderbilt Cup Races. The raceway was built on what previously the eastern end of the Roosevelt Field airport. These two views date to September and October 1936. The bottom one shows the Cup Race in progress. By the time the Mineola Fair moved here, the complex would be fully developed.

A 1936 aerial view of the Cherry Valley Country Club in Garden City shows the Mineola fairgrounds. The three original buildings of Adelphi University's Garden City campus are visible at center left. Also visible at far right is the western end of the Roosevelt Field airport.

A 1946 image of the new Nassau County courthouse that was built on the northern part of the site of the Mineola Fairgrounds.

A c. 1940s image showing the winner of the ox-pulling contest at the fair.

A vintage decal from the Mineola Skating Rink, which was located on the fairground's property south of Old Country Road in the 1930s, '40s, and '50s. The national skating championships were held here in 1955. The rink closed in 1960.

A c. 1940s post card showing the interior of the Mineola Skating Rink—"lighting effect for moonlight number." The note on the back says "Am enclosing a picture of my favorite loafing place for about two nights a week. It's twice as swell as it looks—so help me."

A vintage late 1940s or early 1950s matchbook advertising the Mineola Skating Rink.

Images of the "Baby Show" at the Mineola Fair *circa* late 1940s, where small children were put on display and given prizes for being ... well, you can imagine from the text on this page.

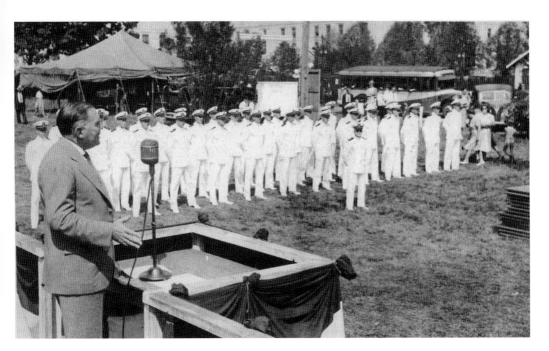

Nassau County Executive J. Russell Sprague delivers the opening address at the fair, *c.* 1951. The new courthouse to the north is in the background.

Various handcrafts have long been staples at the Mineola Fair. Viewing the prizewinning entries has perhaps inspired hundreds or even thousands of visitors to take up a hobby over the years. These images are from *c.* 1951.

The cover of the official 1952 Mineola Fair program. Fair organizers already knew that this would be the last year that the fair would be held in Mineola before moving to Westbury. The size of the fairgrounds had already been reduced by the new courthouse on the northern end, but that was not to be the end of the administrative expansion. Newspapers broke the story of the fair's impending move the next year in March 1952.

Two health-related advertisements in the 1952 Mineola Fair program, offering consultations and free chest x-rays at a time when lung cancer was a bigger threat than today due to excessive smoking, and tuberculosis was still a concern.

A 1952 advertisement from the Drennan Photo Service in Mineola offering to photograph fair exhibits. Led by John Drennan, the Drennan Photo Service was for years one of the most prolific documenters of Long Island life. Originally located at Roosevelt Field, Drennan moved to Mineola in 1951 after the Field permanently closed.

Grandstand Events Program

Tuesday
September 9

8:00 A.M.	Fair Gates open
10:00 A.M.	Exhibits open
1:00 P.M.	Dog Training
2:00 P.M.	Band Concert by Valley Stream High School & Baton Twirling
3:00 P.M.	Band Concert by Oyster Bay High School & Baton Twirling
4:15 P.M.	Ox Pulling & Sheep Dog Herding
7:00 P.M.	Dog Training
8:30 P.M.	Fireworks on Display
8:30 P.M.	Square Dancing at Dance Pavilion
9:00 P.M.	Ox Pulling & Sheep Dog Herding
11:00 P.M.	Fair Exhibits close
Midnight	Midway Carnival closes

Thursday
September 11

8:00 A.M.	Fair Gates open
10:00 A.M.	Exhibits open
12:30 P.M.	Dog Training
1:30 P.M.	Baby Show
2:00 P.M.	Band Concert by Hicksville High School
3:00 P.M.	Band Concert by Sewanhaka High School & Baton Twirling
4:00 P.M.	Band Concert by Sea Cliff High School
5:00 P.M.	Ox Pulling & Sheep Dog Herding
7:00 P.M.	Dog Training
8:30 P.M.	Fireworks on Display
8:30 P.M.	Square Dancing at Dance Pavilion
9:00 P.M.	Ox Pulling & Sheep Dog Herding
11:00 P.M.	Fair Exhibits close
Midnight	Midway Carnival closes

Wednesday
September 10

8:00 A.M.	Fair Gates open
10:00 A.M.	Exhibits open
12:30 P.M.	Dog Training
1:30 P.M.	Baby Show
2:00 P.M.	Band Concert by Malverne High School & Baton Twirling
3:00 P.M.	Band Concert by Mepham High School & Baton Twirling
3:30 P.M.	Ox Pulling & Sheep Dog Herding
7:00 P.M.	Dog Training
8:30 P.M.	Fireworks on Display
8:30 P.M.	Square Dancing at Dance Pavilion
9:00 P.M.	Ox Pulling & Sheep Dog Herding
11:00 P.M.	Fair Exhibits close
Midnight	Midway Carnival closes

Friday
September 12

8:00 A.M.	Fair Gates open
10:00 A.M.	Exhibits open
12:30 P.M.	Dog Training
1:30 P.M.	Band Concert by Pt. Washington High School
2:30 P.M.	Band Concert by Long Beach High School & Baton Twirling
3:30 P.M.	Band Concert by South Side High School & Baton Twirling
4:30 P.M.	Ox Pulling & Sheep Dog Herding
6:00 P.M.	Dog Training
7:30 P.M.	Veterans' Assn. Celebration
8:30 P.M.	Square Dancing at Dance Pavilion
9:45 P.M.	Fireworks on Display
10:00 P.M.	Ox Pulling & Sheep Dog Herding
11:00 P.M.	Fair Exhibits close
Midnight	Midway Carnival closes

Saturday
September 13

8:00 A.M.	Fair Gates open
10:00 A.M.	Exhibits open
12:00 Noon	Dog Training
1:00 P.M.	Crowning Ceremony 4-H King & Queen
2:00 P.M.	Soap Box Derby
4:00 P.M.	Ox Pulling & Sheep Dog Herding
6:00 P.M.	Dog Training
8:30 P.M.	Fireworks on Display
8:30 P.M.	Square Dancing at Dance Pavilion
9:00 P.M.	Ox Pulling & Sheep Dog Herding
11:00 P.M.	Fair Exhibits close
Midnight	MINEOLA FAIR closes for 1952

The program schedule for the 1952 Mineola Fair.

FISH & FOWL at the FAIR

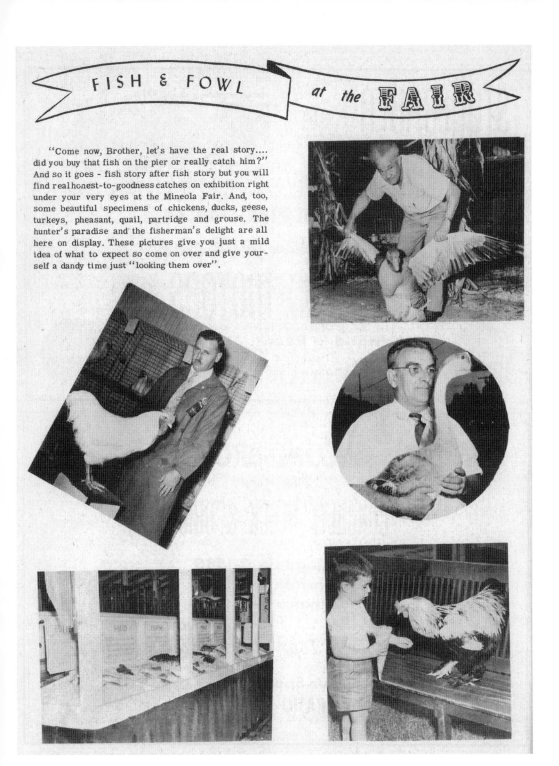

"Come now, Brother, let's have the real story....
did you buy that fish on the pier or really catch him?"
And so it goes - fish story after fish story but you will
find real honest-to-goodness catches on exhibition right
under your very eyes at the Mineola Fair. And, too,
some beautiful specimens of chickens, ducks, geese,
turkeys, pheasant, quail, partridge and grouse. The
hunter's paradise and the fisherman's delight are all
here on display. These pictures give you just a mild
idea of what to expect so come on over and give your-
self a dandy time just "looking them over".

Fish and fowl at the Mineola Fair, a page from the 1952 fair program highlighting some of the many exhibitions.

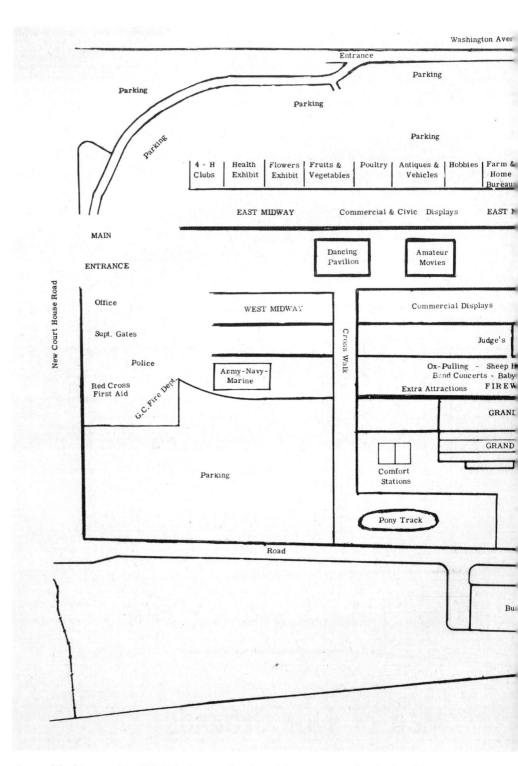

A map of the fairgrounds in 1952, its last year on the site and fourteen years after the size of the grounds had been reduced by the construction of the courthouse on the northern end of the property.

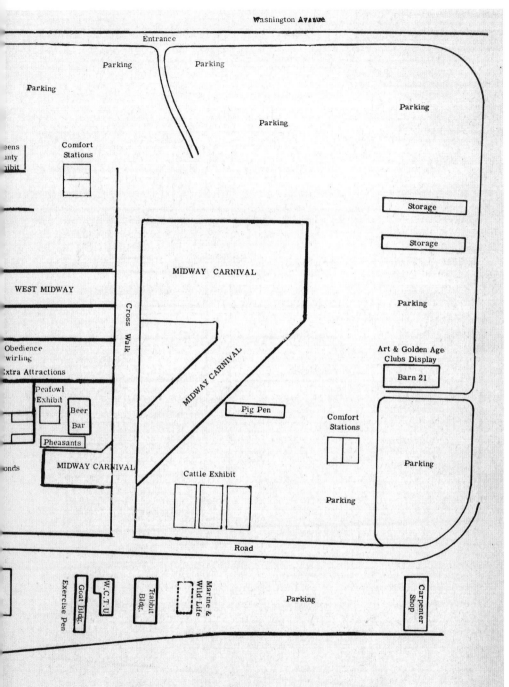

Map of Fair Grounds

Washington Avenue

Entrance

Parking

Parking

Parking

Parking

Parking

Comfort
Stations

Storage

Storage

Parking

MIDWAY CARNIVAL

WEST MIDWAY

Cross Walk

Obedience
Twirling

Extra Attractions

MIDWAY CARNIVAL

Art & Golden Age
Clubs Display

Barn 21

Peafowl
Exhibit

Beer
Bar

Pig Pen

Comfort
Stations

Pheasants

Parking

MIDWAY CARNIVAL

Cattle Exhibit

Parking

Road

Exercise Pen

Goat Bldg.

W.C.T.U

Rabbit
Bldg.

Marine &
Wild Life

Parking

Carpenter
Shop

eens
unty
hibit

onds

A December 1953 aerial view of Mineola shows the now abandoned and defunct fairgrounds, with much of the property still waiting to be developed.

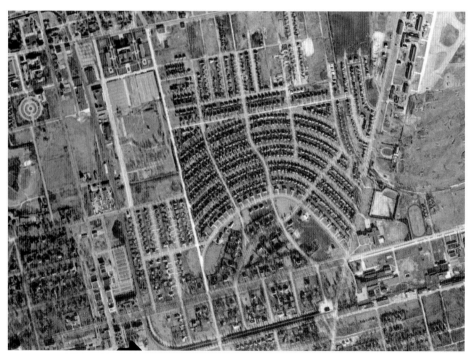

A 1953 aerial view shows the Roosevelt Raceway complex the year it first hosted the Mineola Fair. The remains of the recently closed Roosevelt Field are to the left. Salisbury Park (later to become Eisenhower Park) is to the right.

The Roosevelt Raceway complex offered indoor and outdoor spaces to house fair exhibits and activities. It made sense to move to a venue that also had a racetrack. The fair moved out in 1970 and the complex was abandoned in 1988 after business had slowed over the years, and eventually replaced with retail and residential developments.

OPPOSITE PAGE:

A view of the Roosevelt Raceway complex taken in July 1958, and a color view taken *c.* 1959. The new $20-million Roosevelt Raceway complex, built in 1957, housed the Mineola Fair annually until the fair moved to Old Bethpage in 1970. The building contained 65,000 square feet for exhibitions and was five stories high.

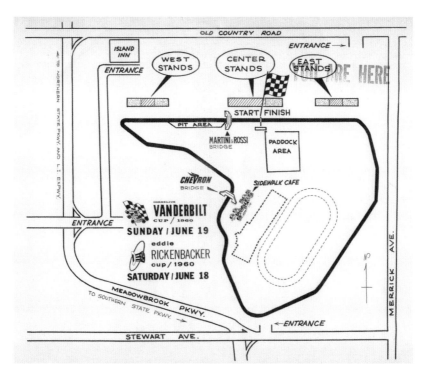

The Mineola Fair was not the only special event held at the Roosevelt Raceway. In 1960 (and previously in 1936/37) the Vanderbilt Cup Races were held there, a direct descendant of the original races that began in the area in 1904 and were named after their creator, the wealthy William K. Vanderbilt, Jr. Shown here is the course map from the 1960 race program.

Long Island potato farmers in a *c.* 1960s photograph. Though farming declined drastically in Nassau County during the twentieth century as land was developed for residential and commercial purposes, agriculture remains a huge industry in Suffolk County to this day—as of 2007, there were 585 farms remaining in Suffolk County, covering 34,404 acres of land.

THE LONG ISLAND FAIR

AGRICULTURAL FAIR - HARNESS RACING
HOOTENANNY - BAND MUSIC - SQUARE DANCING
CARNIVAL - EXHIBITS - CONTINUOUS ENTERTAINMENT

★ **EVERYBODY'S GOING!** ★
ROOSEVELT RACEWAY, Westbury, L. I.

AUGUST 24TH TO SEPTEMBER 2ND
(LABOR DAY)

SPECIAL ROUND TRIP FARES
INCLUDING ADMISSION TO THE LONG ISLAND FAIR
ON THE LONG ISLAND RAIL ROAD
FROM NEW YORK, BROOKLYN AND JAMAICA

FARES FROM NEW YORK & BROOKLYN	FARES FROM JAMAICA
ADULTS — $2.50	ADULTS — $2.00
CHILDREN — $1.50 5 - 11 years	CHILDREN — $1.25 5 - 11 years

FARE INCLUDES TRAIN TO MINEOLA, BUS TO ROOSEVELT RACEWAY, ADMISSION TO THE LONG ISLAND FAIR AND RETURN. TICKETS GOOD ON ALL TRAINS LEAVING NEW YORK, BROOKLYN AND JAMAICA AFTER 10:00 AM.

EXHIBITION HOURS: 11:00 AM TO 11:00 PM DAILY

VISIT THE LONG ISLAND RAIL ROAD EXHIBIT
BOOTHS 189 AND 190

Come to the

LONG ISLAND FAIR
ROOSEVELT RACEWAY
AUG. 24 thru SEP. 2

FaiR

THE LONG ISLAND FAIR
ON THE
LONG ISLAND RAIL ROAD

1963

A Long Island Railroad advertisement for the 1963 Long Island Fair at Roosevelt Raceway. Though Westbury station was closer, this ticket deal had visitors taking the train to Mineola and then a bus to the Raceway.

*...rs flocking to an admission
the Society's new home, Roose-
...way, ticket booths are located
...ounts convenient to spacious
...fields where 12,000 cars
...ndled with ease and dispatch.*

*The men who help make the scene
above a reality—officials of the Agricultural Society of Queens, Nassau
and Suffolk Counties, who meet and
plan throughout the year for each Fair,
consulting with community leaders.*

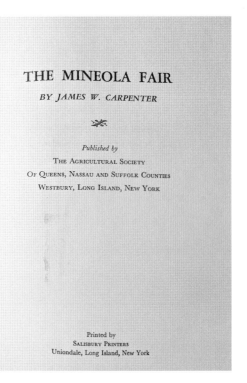

THE MINEOLA FAIR

BY JAMES W. CARPENTER

Published by
THE AGRICULTURAL SOCIETY
OF QUEENS, NASSAU AND SUFFOLK COUNTIES
WESTBURY, LONG ISLAND, NEW YORK

Printed by
SALISBURY PRINTERS
Uniondale, Long Island, New York

In 1965, James W. Carpenter wrote a book about the history of the Mineola Fair, printed by Salisbury Printers of Uniondale and published by the Agricultural Society of Queens, Nassau and Suffolk Counties. Carpenter was self-described as a man who had worn many hats relating to the Fair: "spectator, exhibitor, platform guest, Society member, director, committee member, officer and producer."

A 1966 aerial view shows the former fairgrounds property has now been developed, with the Supreme Court Building occupying the southern portion of the site.

An Old Bethpage Village Restoration graphic from 1970.

A *c.* 1980s image of the fair at its current home in Old Bethpage.

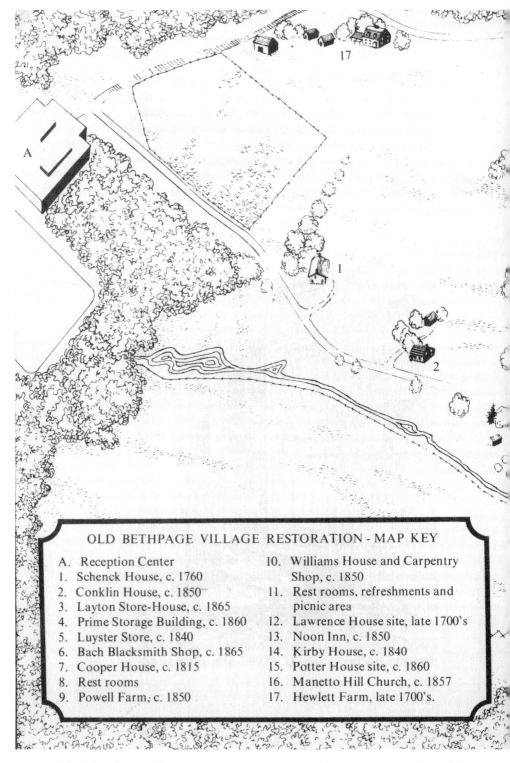

OLD BETHPAGE VILLAGE RESTORATION - MAP KEY

A. Reception Center
1. Schenck House, c. 1760
2. Conklin House, c. 1850
3. Layton Store-House, c. 1865
4. Prime Storage Building, c. 1860
5. Luyster Store, c. 1840
6. Bach Blacksmith Shop, c. 1865
7. Cooper House, c. 1815
8. Rest rooms
9. Powell Farm, c. 1850
10. Williams House and Carpentry Shop, c. 1850
11. Rest rooms, refreshments and picnic area
12. Lawrence House site, late 1700's
13. Noon Inn, c. 1850
14. Kirby House, c. 1840
15. Potter House site, c. 1860
16. Manetto Hill Church, c. 1857
17. Hewlett Farm, late 1700's.

A map of the Old Bethpage Village Restoration as it appeared in 1970, the first year it hosted the Long Island Fair.

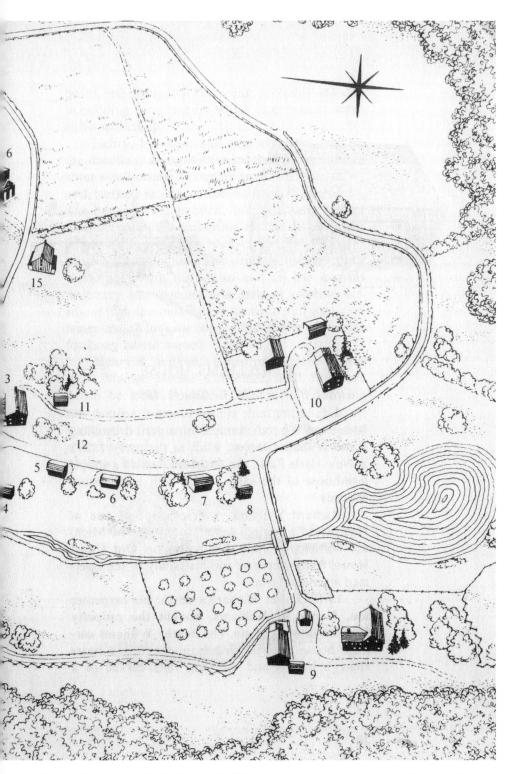

Though fair events are held all across the Village, the main fair location is currently where the map key is and just north of that.

NASSAU COUNTY EXECUTIVE
EDWARD P. MANGANO
Theodore Roosevelt Executive & Legislative Building • 1550 Franklin Avenue, Mineola, NY 11501
Phone: (516) 571-4225 • Fax: (516) 571-4229 • Email: webmangano@nassaucountyny.gov

P R E S S   R E L E A S E

MANGANO ANNOUNCES THE 172ND LONG ISLAND FAIR AT OLD BETHPAGE VILLAGE RESTORATION

Old Bethpage, NY – Nassau County Executive Edward P. Mangano announced today that the Old Bethpage Village Restoration (OBVR) will host the 172nd Annual Long Island Fair over two successive weekends on **Saturday and Sunday, September 27th and 28th and Thursday, October 2nd – Sunday, October 5th**. The Fair, one of America's oldest agricultural festivals, is a family-friendly festival offering a range of attractions, including exotic animals, reptile shows, pony and carnival rides, as well as traditional live music.

Visitors can enjoy magic shows, a petting zoo, and historical entertainment. Stilt walkers traverse the grounds, and entertainers enthrall families with puppets, juggling and storytelling. All of these festivities continue a 172-year tradition. Attractions such as livestock shows, tractor rides, Civil War reenactments, and Rough Rider demonstrations whisk riders back to another era. Visitors will also find:

- **Historical demonstrations:** hat-making, pottery, blacksmithing, weaving, and candle-making;
- **Dance opportunities:** brass bands, a fiddler, bluegrass band Buddy Merriam & Backroads, Homegrown String Band, and kids' singer-songwriter Patricia Shih;
- **For tiny tots:** a Farmer for a Day area and a hands-on Vegetable Orchestra;
- **Tests of skill:** sawing, corn-husking, and scarecrow-building contests; guessing the weight of a giant pumpkin;
- **Tickets required:** rides on camels, ponies, horse-drawn wagons, a hot-air balloon, and a 19th-century carousel; bounce houses;
- **Eats for sale:** candied apples, pumpkins, organic veggies, fresh-made candy, giant turkey legs, and funnel cakes.

Meanwhile, baseball fans can enjoy the end-of-season matches of OBVR's Old Time Baseball League, which recreates "baseball" as it was played in the latter half of the 19th century, with teams competing in authentic uniforms and playing under the names of Long Island clubs of that era.

The Long Island Fair is the New York State-recognized county fair for Queens, Nassau and Suffolk, and involves the cooperation of the Nassau County Department of Parks, Recreation and Museums and the Agricultural Society of Queens, Nassau and Suffolk Counties. Thousands of exhibits are entered every year in friendly competition, with blue ribbon categories including livestock, flowers and vegetables from farms and home gardens, culinary, needlework, hobbies, and a junior division for those 13 and younger. This year's competitions will also include an "Advanced" category for new professionals, novices and students who are serious about their craft. Entries in this category will require a fee, with generous first, second and third place prizes; and the judges will be required to submit credentials in the specific classes.

For the latest news and events occurring in and around Nassau County, please visit
www.nassaucountynewsnetwork.com and/or download the "Nassau Now" app today!

Left: The first page of then County Executive Ed Mangano's press release about the 2014 Long Island Fair.

Below: Looking across the courthouse parking lot in Mineola toward what was once a flying field used by Glenn Curtiss.

A statue of Christopher Columbus stands in roughly the middle of the former Mineola fairgrounds property. The statue was dedicated in 1964 by the Sons of Italy in America.

The "new" Nassau County Courthouse was built on the fairgrounds of former Queens, Nassau Agricultural Society. Planned and constructed as a WPA project in the late 1930s, it opened in 1940. The three-story central unit and two adjacent smaller units housed the County Supreme Courts and other judicial offices replacing the Old Courthouse constructed in 1901, which was repurposed for other administrative uses.

An Art Deco stone eagle sits outside the courthouse. Ground was broken for the building on August 1, 1938, and it was completed in 1940. The new building cost $2.6 million.

A decorative flourish at the Nassau County Courthouse sports a fine coating of verdigris reflecting its age.

Part of the courthouse complex property is covered in grass and from certain vantage points it is possible to imagine you've gone back in time to when the fairgrounds were on the site.

Cherry blossoms in April on the former fairground's property offer a hint of the former bucolic nature of the site before it was turned into a civic center.

Once the Mineola Fair had moved away from the site, that cleared the rest of the property for further development, including the construction of the Nassau Supreme Court Building, seen here from ground level and in an aerial view. The building was completed in 1965 on the southern end of the former fairground's property.

Looking north toward the 1940 Nassau County Courthouse and its two flanking buildings, constructed on the northern portion of the Mineola fairgrounds.

Looking east from the former Mineola Fair site toward what was once the airfield used by Glenn Curtiss in 1909.

Much of the former Mineola Fairgrounds property is taken up by parking lots. This particular lot adjacent to Washington Avenue encompasses the former site of the old racetrack.

Looking northwest from the former site of the Mineola Fairgrounds. The domed old Nassau County Courthouse building is at center left.

The cover of the program for the 2021 Long Island Fair. The fair was not held in 2020 due to the Covid pandemic.

As in days of old, today's Long Island Fair features numerous contests for best produce, from tomatoes, potatoes, and onions to peppers, pumpkins, and gourds. Most of these entries come from backyard gardens rather than farms.

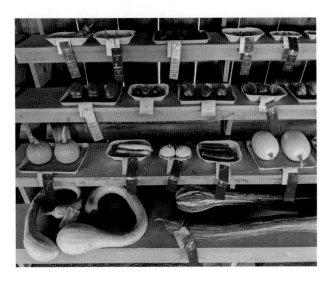

Inside an old general store during the fair, one could purchase a cup of root beer or birch beer for a dollar, or some old-time candy sticks for fifty cents each.

OPPOSITE PAGE:

Above: Though animals were once a larger part of the fair experience, there are still plenty of horses and livestock in the modern version of the fair. Horses such as these are kept in stalls on the edge of the fairgrounds, tended to by their owners and keepers who bring them from far and wide to participate in the fair.

Below: Because of its co-location with the Old Bethpage Village Restoration, the fair can now include some authentic nineteenth-century experiences that had not been possible at the two previous locations. All the buildings in the village were relocated there from elsewhere on Long Island to make a "created" village of genuine vintage buildings, many of which had been in danger of demolition if they'd not been moved.

Fair exhibits inside the main building include art and photography (top) and embroidery and other handcrafts (bottom).

The main fairgrounds building is a modern reconstruction of the nineteenth-century one that stood for decades at the Mineola site. The exposed wood frame of the building is itself a marvel to behold.

Horses on exhibit at the fair can roam in the penned area in the fairgrounds.

Camel rides and pony rides are among the attractions at the fair, which is designed to be family friendly.

A donkey named Hootie was among the animals present at the 2021 Long Island Fair. .

Pumpkin and gourd picking for kids of all ages was just one of the many activities offered at the Long Island Fair.

The Restoration Farm stall offered a variety of produce grown at the Old Bethpage Village.

A variety of performances are featured annually at the Long Island Fair, including bluegrass music, magic, a Punch and Judy puppet show, and a mini circus.

Basket making, broom making, and other crafts are on display in the village during the fair.

Nineteenth-century soldiers dressed in the uniforms of the time were present at the fairgrounds, along with a vintage 35-star American flag.

OPPOSITE PAGE:

Above: Retail and parking lots currently cover much of what used to be the Roosevelt Raceway complex, home of the Mineola Fair from 1953-1970.

Below: The Westbury location of the fair was very close to the spot where Charles Lindbergh's plane became airborne on that day in May 1927 when he set off across the Atlantic Ocean. This view looks west from the spot where his plane became airborne.

The Rottkamp Farm located just off Glen Cove Road in Old Brookville is one of just handful of surviving farms in Nassau County.

Youngs Farm in Glen Head is another surviving farm, offering home grown produce, and country store gifts, and baked goods such as pies.

Meyer's Farm in Woodbury offers an array of fruit, vegetables, and baked goods as well as cut-your-own sunflowers from a vast field.

Though Nassau County farming is almost gone, Suffolk County farming is going strong, with dozens of farms of all types offering everything from apples and peaches to corn and pumpkins. The farm stand pictured is in Cutchogue on the North Fork.

The Queens County Fair is located across the Little Neck Parkway from a suburban residential area in the Glen Oaks neighborhood.

The Queens County Farm Museum held the thirty-eighth Queens County Fair on September 10-12, 2021. The 47-acre farm has been in continuous use since 1697 and is one of the oldest farms in New York State. Though not an officially sanctioned direct descendant of the Mineola Fair that the Long Island Fair is, it is very similar in its scope and offerings.

Looking out at the giant corn maze at the Queens County Fair. The 2021 Amazing Maize Maze was in the shape of a cow inspired by an Andy Warhol artwork.

A four-piece roving band of musicians on stilts was just one of the entertainment acts at the Queens County Fair.

The north side of the fairgrounds hosted a traditional carnival with rides, games, and food vendors.

The Adriance Farmhouse, dating to 1772, is the historic centerpiece of the Queens County Farm Museum.

Similar to the Long Island Fair, the Queens County Fair offers prizes for the best vegetables, flowers, and handcrafts.

A directional sign shows fairgoers where to go at the 2021 Queens County Fair map. The fair was broken into six separate areas, each offering different types of activities.

The Queens County Farm Museum normally has a selection of animals in residence, so fairgoers get the added bonus of enjoying the year-round animal population. As of 2021, the farm had two steer, six sheep, eight goats, two alpaca (one pictured here), two pigs, 150-250 hens, and bees.

The spirit of the original Mineola Fair is alive and well at both the Long Island Fair and the Queens County Fair, both of which will hopefully continue well into the future.